"All over this nation, God is stirring the hearts of men to rise up and enter into their God-given destiny. Lou Turner's lifelong passion is to see men enter into their divine purpose in life. 'Living Life God's Way,' of which this book is a part, is born out of this passion. Throughout this Bible study series, Turner opens up God's Word to help you discover HIS plan for your success in your life, family, and work. If you are ready to get off the treadmill, to begin to enjoy God's fullness in your life and make a significant contribution to the world around you, I recommend that you dive into this life-transforming Bible study."

Hal H. Sacks, D.Min., *BridgeBuilders International Leadership Network*

"It seems North American culture is rapidly moving toward what the Bible calls 'everyone doing what is right in his own mind' (Judges 21:25). The prophet Isaiah declared, 'Woe to those who call evil, good, and good, evil' (Isaiah 5:20). This Bible study series will challenge every man in the 21st century as 'iron sharpens iron'! The Q&As at the end of each chapter really personalize the teaching."

Dennis Conner, *Co-Founder/President, Called to Serve Prayer-Coaching Ministry*

"I have known Lou Turner for over twenty years. Lou loves Jesus and has built his life on the Word of God. Lou's Bible study series, 'Living Life God's Way,' is full of biblical truth that has been tested and can be applied by disciples of Jesus in practical ways. These books will help you grow in your faith and gain confidence and competence, which will increase your fruitfulness in Christ.

Mark Buckley, *Founding Pastor of Living Streams Church*

Living Life God's Way

A Man and His Wife

Lou Turner

A Man and His Wife
First Edition Trade Book, 2020
Copyright © 2020 by Lou Turner

A Man and His Wife is part of the Living Life God's Way Series by Lou Turner.

All rights reserved. No part of this publication may be reproduced, stored in a retrieval system, or transmitted in any form by any means—electronic, mechanical, photocopy, recording, or otherwise—except for brief quotations in critical reviews or articles, without the prior permission of the publisher, except as provided by U.S. copyright law.

Unless otherwise marked, Scriptures are taken from the ESV® Bible (The Holy Bible, English Standard Version®) copyright © 2001 by Crossway Bibles, a publishing ministry of Good News Publishers. ESV Text Edition: 2016. The ESV® text has been reproduced in cooperation with and by permission of Good News Publishers. Unauthorized reproduction of this publication is prohibited. All rights reserved.

Scriptures marked NIV are taken from the Holy Bible, New International Version®, NIV®. Copyright © 1973, 1978, 1984, 2011 by Biblica, Inc.™ Used by permission of Zondervan. All rights reserved worldwide. www.zondervan.com The "NIV" and "New International Version" are trademarks registered in the United States Patent and Trademark Office by Biblica, Inc.™

Scriptures marked TLB are taken from the Living Bible, copyright © 1971. Used by permission of Tyndale House Publishers, Inc., Carol Stream, Illinois 60188. All rights reserved.

Some of the anecdotal illustrations in this book are true to life and are included with the permission of the persons involved. All other illustrations are composites of real situations, and any resemblance to people living or dead is coincidental.

ISBN: 978-1-7331186-2-0

To order additional books:
www.amazon.com
www.hislifeinus.com

Editorial and Book Packaging: Inspira Literary Solutions, Gig Harbor, WA
Book Design: PerfecType, Nashville, TN
Cover Design: MTWdesign, Dickson, TN
Printed in the USA by Ingram Spark

*He will be like a tree firmly planted by streams of water,
Which yields its fruit in its season
And its leaf does not wither;
And in whatever he does, he prospers.*

Psalm 1:3

TABLE OF CONTENTS

Preface   ix

How to Use this Book   xi

Introduction   xiii

1. Loving Your Wife   1

2. Unity: Nothing between You   15

3. Living with Your Wife in Honor and Understanding   25

4. A Husband's Leadership and Authority   41

5. The Responsibility to Provide   59

6. Divorce and Marriage   69

A Final Word   83

About the Author   85

PREFACE

We live in a world that has largely forgotten what manhood is about. In the Western world, men are often portrayed on television as buffoons who are out of touch and must rely on their wives to straighten them out. These characters are portrayed as silly, insensitive, lacking common sense, and when they do speak, they are generally wrong. They are generally portrayed as either ridiculously weak or overly macho. They are not able to commit to a long-term relationship and generally mistreat women. Positive role models are hard to find in the media.

However, the Bible teaches a different type of manhood, the authentic one. Men are to be leaders, loving their wives and children, excelling in their work, and standing for truth. They are to be men of wisdom, knowledge, having godly character and seeking after God and His direction. They are to be exhibiting godly leadership at church, in the community, and in business, and to be a light to those around them. They are to be men of compassion and love, as well as courageous and bold when needed.

Men go astray from these ideals, including Christian men, due to improper convictions or beliefs about life. They have received these from various sources: well-meaning family and friends, the media, and the culture around them—a world system that promotes the tearing down of God's biblical truths.

But without proper biblical foundation, we will all go astray.

PREFACE

That's why I wrote these books, containing insights, observations, and biblical truths distilled over the course of my decades of life and ministry. Each section is designed to be a stand-alone section for study and consideration. I hope this series, *Living Life God's Way*, will be used to disciple men in biblical truths for life. Whether you use it for yourself, with a group, or to mentor or disciple someone else, my hope is that it will be a blessing to you and encourage you to seek God and grow in Him.

HOW TO USE THIS BOOK

What does it mean to be a "good" husband and father?
How do I live out the Christian life at work?
What does God want from me—and how am I supposed to find that out?

These were questions that plagued me as a young man—questions, I learned, that are at the front of many men's minds at various times in their lives. For me, these questions began my quest to seek God and discover the answers, and my discoveries, over the years of my life, led to this series of booklets, *Living Life God's Way*. The series discusses 13 topics that every man must deal with, regardless of his work, calling, profession, or circumstances. It is difficult to know how to live the Christian life without understanding what God says about these areas of life.

These topics are:

1. Seeking and Finding God
2. Who You Are in Christ
3. A Man's Work and Ministry
4. A Man and Authority
5. A Man and His Wife
6. A Man and His Children
7. Getting Guidance from God

8. Overcoming Strongholds
9. A Man and Money
10. Repentance, Forgiveness, and Restitution
11. Being a Leader
12. A Man and Sex
13. The Test of Pride

    You can use these books to study on your own, in a small group, or with a larger group of men. Each topic or booklet is a stand-alone study, and a person can begin with any one he chooses. They are different lengths and can be adapted to various settings—home, church, or community—all topics that are pertinent to today.

    Explore what the Bible says about these important and critical areas. The encouragement is to read these with an open heart, asking God to reveal His truth to you in each of these areas of life. Pray that His Spirit will show you His truth, so that you may live in it and enjoy all God has for you. I pray that you experience the blessing and presence of God in your life as you draw closer to Him and more aware of His leading in every area of your life.

INTRODUCTION TO A MAN AND HIS WIFE

Many relationships in life are important. For those who are married, the Bible teaches that the marriage relationship is second only to our relationship with God and stresses the importance of the marriage relationship. It is an adventure between two people—an adventure God intended to be a rich, loving, and deeply meaningful relationship. Husbands are to love their wives as they love no one else!

It is so important that one of the biblical requirements to hold certain church leadership positions is to have a successful marriage. (This does not mean that a single man cannot be a godly person or qualified for church leadership. The Apostle Paul was single and was certainly qualified to be in church leadership.)

If you are married, or have been married, or want to be married, understanding God's perspective on this relationship is very important. Learning to be a good husband and having a successful marriage requires effort, self-sacrifice, humility, and a great deal of maturing as the marriage progresses. God often uses our marriages to teach us, mature us, and develop us into the men He wants us to be. He works through our marriages to develop godly character traits in us and to teach us to genuinely love and care for another person. This process of learning to live and give sacrificially, and truly loving our wife, causes us to become more Christlike, as those qualities were a part of Christ's life.

On both a Kingdom and personal level, a unified and successful marriage is a positive and influential force in God's economy and the world around us. Those who have successful marriages state without hesitation that on Earth there is no greater source of joy and pleasure than their marriage.

There is a lot to consider in this study and I recommend you take it one part at a time. Don't try to work through it too quickly. Think and pray about each part and allow God to speak to your heart. It's a good practice to pray before you begin each part. Ask God to open your heart and help you hear Him speak to you about what you're reading.

Love is patient, love is kind.

It does not envy, it does not boast, it is not proud.

It does not dishonor others, it is not self-seeking, it is not easily angered, it keeps no record of wrongs.

Love does not delight in evil but rejoices with the truth.

It always protects, always trusts, always hopes, always perseveres.

Love never fails. But where there are prophecies, they will cease; where there are tongues, they will be stilled; where there is knowledge, it will pass away. For we know in part and we prophesy in part, but when completeness comes, what is in part disappears.

When I was a child, I talked like a child, I thought like a child, I reasoned like a child. When I became a man, I put the ways of childhood behind me. For now we see only a reflection as in a mirror; then we shall see face to face. Now I know in part; then I shall know fully, even as I am fully known. And now these three remain: faith, hope and love. But the greatest of these is love.

—1 Corinthians 13:4-13

Chapter 1

LOVING YOUR WIFE

I was praying one day when I sensed the Lord was saying to me, "You cannot love your wife the way she needs to be loved."

I was a bit taken aback as I thought I was doing a pretty good job of loving her. As I continued to pray over these thoughts, I sensed God was saying to me, "Human love always falls short. You need to love her supernaturally." I didn't know what this meant. How could I love someone "supernaturally"? So, I continued to pray and wait on the Lord to communicate further with me.

I began to receive these thoughts: *I want to love Joan through you, and you through her. I want you to be a channel I can love her through. To do that, you need to begin to pray for My supernatural love to be released in you for her, and in her for you. In this way you can begin to experience a supernatural, unconditional love for each other that will be much more fulfilling.* That sounded good to me. Supernatural love? I wanted it.

I began to pray for that love at that moment and have continued to pray since that time. Joan and I also agreed to pray together that God would release His supernatural unconditional love in us for each other. Our love definitely went to another level.

I wish all men would pray for this love for their wives, and pray it will be released in their wives for them. I also wish they would pray for this together with their wives. This is a marriage-changer.

One of the ways God uses marriage is to teach us how to love. I believe every man should memorize 1 Corinthians 13, the famous "love chapter" in the Bible. As you memorize this short chapter of only 13 verses, and meditate on it, it will transform the way you think, relate, and feel about marriage and loving your wife, as well as your children and others. Ephesians 5 is another passage that talks about love, specifically the love a husband is to have for his wife:

> *"Husbands, love your wives, just as Christ loved the church and gave himself up for her to make her holy, cleansing her by the washing with water through the word, and to present her to Himself as a radiant church, without stain or wrinkle or any other blemish, but holy and blameless. In this same way, husbands ought to love their wives as their own bodies. He who loves his wife loves himself. After all, no one ever hated their own body, but they feed and care for their body, just as Christ does the church." (Ephesians 5:25-29)*

God loves us and wants us to learn to love others. God gave sacrificially to us, and wants us to learn to give sacrificially to others—especially our wives. One of the greatest challenges most of us face in this is selfishness. Another is expecting our mate to live up to a standard that may be unrealistic or even unscriptural. First Peter 3:8-12 says,

> *"Finally, all of you, be like-minded, be sympathetic, love one another, be compassionate and humble. Do not repay evil with evil or insult with insult. On the contrary, repay evil with blessing, because to this you were called so that you may inherit a blessing. For, 'Whoever would love life and see good days must keep their tongue from evil and their lips from deceitful speech. They must turn from evil and do good; they must seek peace and pursue it. For the eyes of the Lord are on the righteous and his ears are attentive to their prayer, but the face of the Lord is against those who do evil.'"*

As men, part of our leadership role is to confront this selfishness, to set a different tone for our marriage and establish a positive family culture as we love our wives with God's love. Following are some of the things the Bible says we are to pursue as we love our wives.

Delight in Your Wife

The Bible speaks of a love between a man and a woman that does not "wear out" or "get old." It continues to be a rich and exciting relationship throughout our lives. Many believe this is not possible, but the Bible says it is. Please read Proverbs 5:15-23 and the Song of Solomon. Here you will see a man and woman loving each other and seeking each other out romantically.

For a man, this happens by a husband choosing to love and cherish his wife, treating her with love, respect, and honor, and choosing to delight in her. When we view our wives this way, it is amazing how the quality and dynamics of the relationship change.

Wives, on their part, are also responsible for learning to delight in or cherish their husbands and treat them with love, respect, and honor. When a couple does this, the whole dynamic of their marriage shifts and the whole atmosphere of their home changes.

Actions and attitudes will begin to transform as we daily determine to think of our spouses in this way. Focusing on perceived shortcomings or things we want to change in each other only produces frustration for both. A much better emphasis is loving and delighting in each other, valuing and looking for the good in one another.

To do this, both the husband and wife should bring to mind the positive things the other brings into the relationship. Doing this brings the romance and qualities into the relationship that we all desire and secretly hope for in our marriage. There is no need to go elsewhere.

Think about it. How did you think of your wife when you were pursuing her? Did you concentrate on her shortcomings and weaknesses? Or were you excited to be with her and concentrate on her good qualities?

But, you might say, *I didn't know her then like I do now.* How true. But how does God know you? Is there anything He does not know about you? And yet He loves you—in spite of your shortcomings, weaknesses, and failures. He sees your potential and wants you to grow and develop into the person He sees you can be. His Spirit encourages you to become that person, and His motivation is His love for you.

In the same way, we should love our wives and want them to be all that God wants them to be (realizing that this may be different from what we want them to be!). By loving your wife, encouraging her, and praying for her, you will help her to grow into that person. It's best to allow God to take over and develop your wife instead of you trying to do the job. I guarantee you will like the results much more. So will she.

There is no doubt that real problems exist in marriages, problems that need to be resolved. However most, if not all, become resolvable when a husband and wife determine to truly *love* one another. Loving each other and wanting to please God means each spouse is willing to talk about issues, pray about them, and ask God to get involved in their marriage.

As we invite God into our problems and seek His will for their resolution, He does just that. He gets involved. In James 1:5 it says, *"If any of you lacks wisdom, he should ask God, who gives generously to all without finding fault, and it will be given to him."* If we are open, and ask for God's wisdom and direction, He will give it.

Pray for Your Wife

We generally underestimate the power and effectiveness of prayer. I like what one man said, "Prayer is the lubrication of the Holy Spirit." Prayer releases God's Spirit to go to work. When we pray we are calling on God to help us, give us wisdom and direction, and ask for His will to be done. God delights in our praying to Him. He responds to prayer.

Unfortunately, most of us do not have a regular and consistent prayer life—I mean the kind where we set aside time daily to be alone with God, in a place by ourselves, where we pray and seek Him. Consistent prayer changes us and changes our circumstances. It changes the course of our life, our outlook on life, and what we accomplish in life. It is our daily lifeline to God.

Jesus needed to pray. He would spend all night in prayer at times (Mark 1:35, 6:46; Luke 6:12, 15:16). He needed time with His Father, God. So do we. Whether we really realize it or not, we really need regular time with Him. Jesus was the greatest man that ever lived and He realized His need to spend time with God, His Father, regularly. We are not as great as Him and yet we think we can get along on our own. I think there is something wrong here. We need to acknowledge our need to spend time with God and then do it; regularly and daily.

As men, being the best husband we can be, and being a leader in our home, means praying for our wives and children. Amazing things can happen as we regularly pray for our wives, our marriage, and our family. Get God involved in your marriage. Pray Him into it. Ask Him for His will, His insight, His purpose, His plan, and His presence. Ask Him to change you where you need to be changed; to renew your mind and change your heart.

During your prayer times alone, pray for your wife as well. This may include asking God to change her in the areas where He wants to change her. But be open to Him changing *you* first! He knows what needs to be done. Bathing a marriage in prayer is powerful and will bring positive change as needed.

God sees things differently than we do. When we begin to pray, He often gives us insights we need. Many times, His thoughts are much different than ours. But His thoughts are truth and bring life into any situation.

Respect Your Wife

Mutual respect is essential in any successful relationship; in marriage, it is especially essential. Webster defines respect as, "Honor shown to others for their good qualities or worth. Treating others with esteem, good favor, and high regard." A "best practice" for husbands and wives is to treat each other with the highest possible respect.

Naturally, people are imperfect and bring their imperfections into marriage. There will be disagreements, and in some cases, strong disagreements. Since we are different people, at times we will want to do things differently than each other. That is normal. However, each party must keep in mind that God intends us to learn to love each other, be patient with one another, and treat one another with respect. If there is a commitment to loving and respecting each other, resolution of differences will follow.

Giving respect to our mate is part of love. It means we listen, we value, and we give importance to her and her opinions. We do not speak to her or about her in a condescending manner. In addition, if we have children, they learn to respect their mother by the respect their father shows her. It is important that a husband never show disrespect to his wife in front of his children, nor should he allow his children to show disrespect to her. Deal with issues you have with your wife in private. Mutual respect should always be shown in the presence of all others.

I knew a man who said condescending things about his wife in front of others, and would then laugh. I could see she was embarrassed and hurt. Finally after years of disrespectful behavior from him toward her, she left him for another man. He realized, over time, he had chased her away and began to seek God about his wife and marriage. She eventually came back after he humbled himself and began to seek her out. It took time, months, before she became convinced he was sincere and had a genuine heart change.

At first she didn't want anything to do with him. She was hurt and had given up on him and their marriage. She had to be willing to open her heart and allow God to heal her emotionally. But first the husband had to allow God to change him and be repentant over his actions and attitudes toward her. God responded to both of them as they sought Him and restored their marriage. It could have easily gone the other way.

Showing genuine respect, listening to your wife, and loving her are essential to a successful relationship.

Encourage Your Wife

Words and attitudes are powerful. They have the power to build up and to tear down. That's why we receive such a strong exhortation in Ephesians 4:29: *"Do not let any unwholesome talk come out of your mouths, but only what is helpful for building others up according to their needs, that it may benefit those who listen."*

Proverbs tells us the very power of life and death is in our words: *"Death and life are in the power of the tongue, and those who love it will eat its fruit"* (Proverbs 18:21).

Along those lines, the Apostle James reminds us of the seriousness of what we communicate: *"We all stumble in many ways. Anyone who is never at fault in what they say is perfect, able to keep their whole body in check"* (James 3:2). In other words, control your tongue and speak what is good to build up others.

Even if we need to deal with tough situations or difficult topics, it should be done in such a manner that the end result is not a tearing down of the other person but a building up (and this goes for all relationships, not just marriages). Our motive should always be to encourage and bring healing, to honor and build worth.

If we are dealing with tough issues, the purpose is to understand and help our mate. If our motive is just to get our own way or win the argument, then we have already lost because we will end up bringing discouragement and causing a barrier in the relationship.

Obviously, there are times in many relationships when correction is necessary to put a person on the right path or bring correct thinking. The purpose is to speak truth, build up, and protect.

Even when forceful correction may become necessary, it is to stop people from being hurt or hurting themselves or others.

A husband should also encourage his wife to develop her gifts and talents, within their financial means. All people need to grow and develop in life, and not get stuck in a rut. This will not only bring her fulfillment, but will also enrich the marriage and family. As each person in the marriage relationship grows personally and shares their journey with the other, both grow together. Examples of this might be classes to develop a talent or ability, or an encouragement to get involved in ministry activities in church or in the community. (Of course, for both husbands and wives, developing talents and gifts should not interfere with the other priorities of marriage and family. Growing and developing our talents and abilities is good, but no one should pursue their own interests to the point it causes neglect of our marriage or family—or any other God-given priorities, for that matter.)

Protect Your Wife

Since a man is normally physically stronger than his wife, out of love he will want to protect her. That being said, protecting her involves not only physical protection, but also protecting her emotionally and protecting her reputation.

A man should never say demeaning things about his wife either to her or behind her back. He should never reveal intimate details about their relationship or speak openly about her faults to others. If a man is seeking counsel, there may be a need to bring up some of these topics, but only to a trusted counselor or friend who will not repeat the information being shared. And then, it is to get wise counsel to further your relationship with your wife, not to get someone on your side against her.

Part of a husband's role as protector is also to protect his wife from an unhealthy environment or relationship. Perhaps your wife is in an unhealthy work environment. Take this on in prayer as a couple; lend your leadership and support to her concerns, and together start to seek God's wisdom and direction and pray for a change.

Additionally, don't let anxiety over finances cause you to compromise your role of protector. Your wife is more valuable than money. Keep in mind that "[Love] *always protects*, always trusts, always hopes, always perseveres" (1 Corinthians 13:7, emphasis added). It is God who provides all your needs. He can provide a new job—either yours or your wife's (Philippians 4:13).

Keep the Fire Burning

Proverbs 5:18 says, *"May your fountain be blessed, and may you rejoice in the wife of your youth."* Do you remember what first attracted you to your wife, and her to you? No doubt you spent many hours learning about one another and enjoying each other's company. There was usually no obstacle too big to overcome in order to spend time together.

But after the wedding, new responsibilities set in and real life tends to take over. Our commitments and responsibilities at work, our children, extended family, church commitments, and other priorities can rob our marriage of the love and romance it needs to thrive. If we're not careful, those fires of attraction and connection can dwindle.

It *is* possible for a husband and wife to lose their relationship in the midst of the activities of their own family. Remember, God ordained the marriage first, then the family. Both husband and wife must keep the fire burning by taking time for each other and honoring that priority in their lives. For this reason, it is imperative to continue to pursue your wife. This means dating her, spending time alone with her, being intimate with her, and showing her you love and value her.

A weekly date night can be a lifesaver in this department. If your children are small, make it your responsibility to find a babysitter, set aside the needed finances for the evening, and make it happen. Your wife will feel treasured.

When Joan and I were young and at a low point financially, I was seeking God and He was moving in my life. A mentor began to encourage me to date my wife weekly even though we had small children and little extra money. We took walks in the park, ate at cheap restaurants, and just spent time together. It was a godsend for both of us. She needed time away from the children with me, and I needed time with just her. These times caused our relationship to continue to grow and kept the fire burning. We needed to talk and be together. We needed to keep our bond strong.

Date nights are just as important when your children are grown. Many times a husband and wife go through an identity crisis of sorts when children leave home. They need to rediscover each other and re-establish their relationship. It is better to keep the relationship solid along the way. Sadly, many marriages do not make it at this point. Taking trips alone and spending time together is essential to keeping the marriage healthy.

Date your wife, take her away on romantic weekends, take walks, and spend time with her. If money is tight, you can still go to cheap movies or inexpensive restaurants, and pray for God to supply money for getaways. At times a man needs to plan this out, including arranging childcare, to give the wife a break from having to do everything at home. This will also show her he values her and their time together. Don't let life steal your relationship. Keep the fire burning!

Loving as God Would Have Us Love

As mentioned earlier, 1 Corinthians 13:4-5 is a passage worthy of our memorization. It says,

> *Love is patient, love is kind. It does not envy, it does not boast, it is not proud. It does not dishonor others, it is not self-seeking, it is not easily angered, it keeps no record of wrongs.*

Most of us have to learn to love the way God wants us to. We initially fall in love. But then we need to learn to love God's way. Most of us have to *learn* to love this way. It is part of growing as a person. Meditating on this passage and others like it will help plant in our hearts and minds the meaning of love; it will teach us how to love. Remember, God desires for us to learn to love our mates as He intends; therefore, He will help us as we ask Him to.

QUESTIONS FOR REFLECTION AND DISCUSSION

Ask yourself the following questions regarding your marriage.

1. Am I happy with my marriage? If not, why?

    _____
    _____
    _____
    _____

2. Is my wife happy with our marriage? (You need to ask her, and allow her to be honest with no fear of your anger or backlash if she is honest.) What is her answer?

3. After reading the above scriptures and thoughts about marriage, are there areas I need to change? If so, what are they?

4. What will be my course of action regarding these things?

5. What qualities do I admire in my wife?

6. Am I an encouragement to her? Do I give her praise and respect her? If so, how?

TAKE A KNEE

Let's kneel to God in prayer, inviting God to take a central place in your marriage. If you are unable to kneel physically, then kneel in your heart. *"Dear Father, I want my marriage to be all You want it to be. I surrender myself, my wife, and our marriage to You. I ask You now to take the central place in our relationship. I ask You to draw me into prayer for my wife and marriage, and to give me wisdom. Show me the things You desire me to see. Give me the insights You desire me to have. Transform my marriage into a marriage that is pleasing to You. Teach me how to love my wife the way You desire."*

Chapter 2

UNITY:
NOTHING BETWEEN YOU

God Himself instituted marriage. He ordained that a man and woman would come together and be unified in marriage:

The LORD God said, "It is not good for the man to be alone. I will make a helper suitable for him." . . . But for Adam no suitable helper was found. So the LORD God caused the man to fall into a deep sleep; and while he was sleeping, he took one of the man's ribs and then closed up the place with flesh. Then the LORD God made a woman from the rib he had taken out of the man, and he brought her to the man.

The man said, "This is now bone of my bones and flesh of my flesh; she shall be called 'woman,' for she was taken out of man." For this reason a man will leave his father and mother and be united to his wife, and they will become one flesh. (Genesis 2:18, 21-24)

God blessed this union of a man and a woman: *"Then God saw everything that He had made, and indeed it was very good"* (Genesis 1:31). The way God made man and the way God made woman was very good. He made no mistakes. The union of man and woman was also very good and God was pleased. The way God made man and woman—physically, mentally, spiritually, emotionally, and sexually—and His purposes for marriage—were all "very good."

Jesus, in Matthew 19:4-6, restated the importance of marriage:

"Haven't you read," he replied, "that at the beginning the Creator made them male and female, and said, 'For this reason a man will leave his father and mother and be united to his wife, and the two will become one flesh'? So they are no longer two, but one flesh. Therefore what God has joined together, let no one separate."

It is obvious from these scriptures that God intended for marriage to be a permanent, life-long bonding together of a man and a woman. "What God has joined together, *let no one separate*" (emphasis added). It was a relationship He wanted to be sustained and blessed.

Beyond that, marriage is not just an experiment. It is a covenant entered into between a man, a woman, and God. Since God ordained it, we are entering into what He has ordained and desires to bless. Thus it is a three-way covenant; a man and woman entering into a God-ordained marriage, and asking God to bless their union.

The mystery of being "one flesh" is only understood in the context of marriage between a man and a woman. A husband and wife are to share life, become a family, produce children (if they are able and choose to), learn to love each other and their children, face life's challenges together, and grow in their relationship with each other and with God.

This is the "one-flesh" experience God was speaking about. Not only are they to "know" each other physically through sexual relations, but also they are to know each other more intimately than any other person. As a husband and wife go through life and its challenges, God wants them to stand together in unparalleled unity, seek Him, renew their commitment, grow in their love, and learn the joy and meaning of marriage.

Nothing between You

A husband is the one who "will leave his father and mother and be united to his wife" (Matthew 19:5). His wife becomes his most important relationship. He must guard the relationship with his wife and let nothing come between them.

Jesus said no one is to come between the husband and wife (19:6). This means **no person, institution, circumstance, or other relationship should be allowed to create disunity in the marriage. This includes friends and family. We all—both husbands and wives—must be on guard to prevent this from happening.**

Choosing to love your wife and to let nothing come between you and her is just that—a choice. It is one we all have to make every day as things try to come between our wife and us. The devil is like the thief Jesus spoke of in John 10:9 who comes to "steal, kill, and destroy." This is particularly true in marriage, where the enemy often finds it very effective to bring disunity to the relationship with a divide-and-conquer strategy.

Men, it is *our* responsibility as *leaders* in our marriages, to *ensure* this does not happen! When we become aware that it is happening, we should renew our commitment to our wife, our marriage and our love for our wife. Taking leadership this way is a strong step to making sure our marriages are successful, joyful, and meaningful.

We cannot let even our family or extended family members come between us. I knew of a young couple where the husband's family was quite critical of his wife in the early years of their marriage. She was a quiet person and was intimidated by his family, who were very outgoing. They mistook this for not being friendly and thought she didn't care for them.

The husband tried to explain, but they continued their criticism. Finally, the young husband had to take a stand. He told his family that he did not want to hear any more criticism of his wife. He loved her and she was a good partner. This put a stop to their criticism in his presence. Remember: constructive criticism is one thing; a critical spirit is another.

Also note that not all things that can divide your relationship and create disunity between you are necessarily bad in and of themselves. For example, children can be allowed to come between a husband and wife if they are idolized or catered to beyond what is appropriate in God's plan for the family. The same would be true of friendships, extended family relationships (including the in-laws), etc. Even church or helping others can be allowed to get to a point of excess where the marriage and family are neglected. You and your wife are a team, and the marriage team should take priority over all other relationships and commitments.

In addition, a husband's personal interests can disrupt his marriage. I saw this in Joe, who was a likeable man and had been successful in his business. He and his wife had married relatively young and they had four sons. They had attended the same evangelical church for many years.

Joe was also a football fanatic. He would spend all day Saturday watching college football, and, after church, all day Sunday watching professional football. And, of course, there was Monday and Thursday night football. In prayer for him one day, I felt impressed to talk to him about his personal walk with the

Lord and his relationship with his wife. I felt deeply impressed that God was saying Joe needed to change his priorities or he was going to lose both his wife and his business.

The following week I asked him about his daily time of prayer and Bible study. He said that he was so busy he didn't always have time to set aside for time alone with God. Rather, he would pray in the car or as he felt a need to do so. I encouraged him to set aside time with the Lord as a priority each day. I also talked to him about the amount of time he spent watching football and television.

Joe told me he loved football. After working hard all week, that was how he liked to spend his weekends. I asked him about time with his wife and sons. Was he spending some of his weekend with them? He assured me all was well on the home front. I then shared with him the impressions that I had received about his time, his priorities, and his wife. He laughed and told me I was off base. He felt no need for a change. Two years later, however, his wife left him for another man. He went bankrupt and lost almost everything.

All that to say: If we are not willing to order our time and priorities as we should, our circumstances may change our priorities for us!

This story illustrates the truth that we must be stewards of our time. I enjoy sports and watching them on TV. I have played team and individual sports much of my life. I loved to play basketball and softball after college on my church team and in pickup games. I was captain of my high school basketball team and enjoyed playing football.

However, as I have thought and prayed about this over the years, my appetite for spending hours watching sports on TV every week has changed. Some time for recreational TV may be okay for most. But if we like to watch sports, we must assess how much time we should spend watching it and when it gets to the point we are neglecting our families.

We need to be open to God's leading in this area. We didn't become husbands and fathers to abandon our families for any activity—including sports, our work, watching television, or our hobbies. A man needs to have an outlet for his interests. Time spent hunting, fishing, in the outdoors, playing sports or pursuing areas of interest can be good, but spending too much time to the neglect of our families is not good. Willfully neglecting our marriage and children is sin against them. It is neglecting our God-given priorities.

Making this area a matter of prayer and asking God to show us His will is not only wise, it may save us great heartache. Pray about your time and activities. There may be things in your life the Lord wants you to take on or drop off for the sake of your marriage. This is also a good area to discuss with your wife and be open to her input. Remember, all that you have belongs to God, including your time. We need to use it wisely as He would have us to.

A Strategy to Work through Tough Spots

Life presents problems and heartache at times. Every marriage will hit one or more crisis points. These crisis points will determine whether we grow closer and more in love, or whether our relationship will diminish and perhaps, ultimately fail.

When Joan and I were married, both of us assumed we would be married for life. However, we did not anticipate the problems and challenges we would encounter, or how they could tear our marriage apart if we allowed them to. As time passed and challenges came, we stayed together, prayed, sought God, and then watched Him work in our lives and marriage. We grew, our unity grew, our love grew, and our lives were richer for it.

Developing a strategy to deal with conflict is essential to a unified marriage. A couple must have a way to approach these problems that will bring resolution and a stronger union. Screaming and fighting (or, on the passive end, withholding and the "silent treatment") are never positive ways to resolve issues. When crisis hits, you and your wife first need to affirm to each other that you're both in this relationship for life and that you *will* work through this crisis together.

A simple object lesson may help illustrate this truth: When you are feeling divided in your relationship, think about the issue or issues that you are dealing with. It may help to imagine the source of your difficulty as a three-dimensional object. You can even choose a tangible object to represent your problem when you and your wife sit down together to discuss (and, hopefully, pray about) it.

Start with the object between the two of you, representing the problem or issue you are dealing with. State your resolve that this difficulty is *not* going to come between you. Then physically move the object away from you and emphatically declare before the Lord, and one another that this issue will not divide you. Rather, the reality of the situation is that you and your wife are united against the problem and all the ways the enemy is seeking to bring disunity to your relationship through it. Affirm this. Declare it. Then tackle the problem or issue together.

Here are some ways to do that:

- Talk about it. Both husband and wife should share their feelings and viewpoints.
- Discuss the differences. Listen to each other and consider each other's perspective.
- Look at the problem in light of Scripture.
- Pray about the problem and ask God for wisdom. Open your hearts and ask God to give you both His insight and

perspective. If it is a difficult problem, try to pray together about it every day.
- Ask God to change your hearts as needed. This is essential. If we are not open to change and are not willing to allow God to deal with us and change our hearts, there cannot be any growth. Giving God permission to change your heart, or better yet, giving your heart to God and ask Him to do as He will, can be a bit scary. *What does that mean? What will He do?* Keep in mind that God loves us and will only work to build us up. He will change us for the better. He will always do what we need and what is for our good. We will become more joyful and peaceful and enjoy our life more because of His work in us.
- Seek godly counsel. If you are unable to resolve the issue, seek out those you know will give you practical and scriptural counsel.
- Determine to love and respect one another while working through the problems. Purpose to maintain loving attitudes and give each other the highest possible respect in the process.

It is a good idea for you and your wife to write down your strategy for resolving conflict in your marriage. That way, when conflict comes, you can go to your strategy, re-read it, and practice what you have committed to do in order to resolve conflict. **If you are committed to resolving problems, praying together, being obedient to Scripture, seeking God with an open heart for His answers, and then following His leading, things will almost certainly get resolved.** His plan for your marriage is unity, and for our marriage to grow stronger. His guidance will lead to a blessed life and marriage.

For marriage to be all it can, God must be involved. He is the third cord in the "threefold cord" spoken of in Ecclesiastes 4:9-12.

With Jesus Christ as the binding element of your marriage, the union of husband and wife can withstand all the onslaughts the enemy, the lies of this world, and the difficulties that the circumstances of life can throw at you.

> *Two are better than one, because they have a good return for their labor: If either of them falls down, one can help the other up. But pity anyone who falls and has no one to help them up. Also, if two lie down together, they will keep warm. But how can one keep warm alone? Though one may be overpowered, two can defend themselves. A cord of three strands is not quickly broken.* (Ecclesiastes 4:9-12).

QUESTIONS FOR REFLECTION AND DISCUSSION

1. Are you allowing "anything" to come between you and your wife? If so, what is it and what is your future course of action concerning it?

   _____
   _____
   _____

2. Are you willing to submit your time to God and seek Him for His will and wisdom of how to use it? List any areas where you are aware that change is needed?

   _____
   _____
   _____

3. Has your wife suggested there are things you need to make more time for? If so, what response do you sense God would have you give her?

_____

_____

_____

4. Have you and your wife agreed on a strategy to resolve differences? If so, what is it? If not, are you willing to talk with her about this?

_____

_____

_____

TAKE A KNEE

Let's pray: *"Father, please show me any areas where I need to guard the unity with my wife that You desire for us. I do not want to let anything come between us. Show me the areas where I am not using my time wisely. When it comes to my marriage or family, reveal to me the things I need to be aware of when it comes to my time with them. May Your Spirit lead me and prod me to use my time as I should. Show me how to resolve differences with my wife. Give me the conviction I need to follow through. Change my heart as needed."*

Chapter 3

LIVING WITH YOUR WIFE IN HONOR AND UNDERSTANDING

When Joan and I were first married, we were very much in love. But, as a young man, I was both strong-willed and very opinionated about how our lives should be lived. I was surprised when my wife disagreed with me and did not think as I did. Though I always loved her, I spent a number of years trying to "mold" my wife in "my image."

One day in prayer, it occurred to me that God had made her as *He* liked, and by not allowing her to be the person He wanted her to be, I was not only hurting her but hindering God's intention for her and our marriage. I began to realize her differences of opinion were often good insight for me. In addition, her talents and abilities added a great deal to our marriage. Together we were stronger, more talented, and more gifted than I was alone.

This was a real "Aha!" experience for me. After I had this realization and released her to be herself, she began to grow, blossom, and develop into the person God wanted her to be—not necessarily the person I originally thought she should be, but better. God did a much better job than I did! I can't express the blessing she has been to my life.

Honor Differences

Part of loving our wives is to understand and honor them in our actions, attitudes, and thoughts. In 1 Peter 3:7, the Apostle Peter exhorts men, "Likewise, husbands, live with your wives in an understanding way, showing honor to the woman as the weaker vessel, since they are heirs with you of the grace of life, so that your prayers may not be hindered."

In this passage, Peter reminds us that, by God's design, women are a more delicate creation, and we should therefore treat them with consideration and respect. The word "weaker" in this passage is not referring to our wives' talents, abilities, intelligence, or spiritual gifts, all of which are given equally to both men *and* women. In fact, there are things our wives can do better than we can, just as there are things we can do better than our wives. Giving consideration to our wife because of her gender is not an issue of talents or abilities. Women are generally weaker than men physically and often more sensitive emotionally—both of which help us to develop as men as we learn to consider and love our wives, and adapt to them.

This principle is also *not* an issue of equality. Galatians 3:27-28 says, *"For as many of you as were baptized into Christ have put on Christ. There is neither Jew nor Greek, there is neither slave nor free, there is no male and female, for you are all one in Christ Jesus."* This passage states that God looks at men and women equally; both have equal value and purpose in His plan. Even though He purposed to make them different, one is not less than the other.

It is difficult for some to distinguish between the roles God identified for men and women and also embrace the equality God intended. Men are generally stronger physically and, usually, emotionally, and are called to lead in the marriage. Women are called to choose to submit to their husbands' leadership. But none of these mean that in God's sight women are less important than men or are subservient to men. As husbands, we are to accord our wives *all* the value and honor that God gives to them and wants them to have.

A demonstration of honoring our wives is that we do not demand them to be just like us. Recognize and celebrate that God made men and women differently! In general, women are more right-brained than men. They tend to be more emotionally intuitive and expressive and often see things through a different filter.

Biologically, women are also different. This biological difference often causes them to have different priorities than men. The home, children, and preserving the family are generally strong motivators in a woman. As you love your wife and communicate with her, you will see these priorities come out of her heart. Though they may be different at times from your priorities, they are good and necessary to the development of your family and to society in general.

At the same time, men should not demean themselves because they are different than women. In our society today—especially in the media—it often seems that men are put down just because they are men and are different from women. This is wrong. Men are to be men and women are to be women. God created both. He likes manhood and womanhood. They were His idea!

Men, we should not apologize for being men. Manhood is not only good, it is essential for a healthy marriage, family, and society. Society today wants men to be more like women, and vice versa. This is not God's plan. He wants us to be the kind of man He wants us to be. But still men! Scripture tells us, *"Be on your guard; stand firm in the faith; be men of courage; be strong. Do everything in love"* (1 Corinthians 16:13-14). The Living Bible version states, *"Keep your eyes open for spiritual danger; stand true to the Lord; act like men; be strong; and whatever you do, do it with kindness and love."*

The bottom line is that both genders should honor one another and respect their unique qualities and contributions. Neither should put the other down if they make a mistake, have a different opinion, or because they are different than us.

Understand Your Wife

The Apostle Peter also emphasized that husbands are to live with their wives in "an understanding way" (1 Peter 3:7). Understanding your wife is not the impossible task some might make it seem. We can begin by realizing that, often, our wives will think differently and see things differently than us. Even when they agree, their perspective may be different from ours.

Accepting this and seeing it as a strength and not a detriment in your marriage is an essential beginning. If you expect your wife to always think like you and see everything as you do, you are in for a rude awakening!

Also, bear in mind that you and your wife entered into marriage with different backgrounds, expectations, dreams, aspirations, and hopes. You came from different families who approached things differently in many areas and now this must be blended into a new family. This is where an openness to healthy compromise and striving to please each other are essential.

As the years go on, understanding each other can take on new meaning and dimension as we grow and change our thinking about things. Your circumstances change, children come, and your career(s) take new turns. Communicating, understanding, and respecting each other through the seasons of life are keys to a successful marriage.

Practically, the first step to understanding your wife is to talk to her and seek out her perspective. If you don't understand it or you disagree, try to find out why she thinks or feels as she does.

> *In marriage, there will not always be agreement, but there can be harmony.*

Spend time with her. Ask questions. Seek her opinions. This will help you understand how she thinks and feels about things. Communication is a huge issue in marriage. If you can talk, listen, *and* communicate (it isn't always a given that talking necessarily means real communication or understanding is occurring), it helps dispel misunderstandings.

If a husband offends his wife by not listening to her, seeking her counsel, and valuing her opinion, then she will not feel important to him. Remember, one of the reasons God gave a wife to Adam was to complete him (Genesis 2:18). This means a wife's perspective and opinions are important, and a husband should listen to and respect them, just as your wife should listen to and respect yours.

This does not mean we stop having our own opinions. It also doesn't mean we become weak-willed and indecisive. Rather, we get input of our wife's opinions, thoughts, and impressions, and consider all sides.

At times, after considering all, we may decide to move forward with our original direction. At other times, we may change our minds. Regardless, we make decisions based upon the best wisdom and input we have—including that of our wife. Our wives feel valued when they are listened to and we value their counsel. You might be surprised how your relationship with her will change when she believes you value her and her input.

If it is an important decision, especially if there is disagreement, pray—both with your wife and alone. Seek God's wisdom and refuse to move forward until you have a peace in your spirit about your direction. If you and your wife are praying with an open heart, God will either give you peace about direction, or a lack thereof, to both of you. Agreement can be an important safeguard against making a wrong decision.

Remember, if we fail to honor our wives and live in an understanding way with them, our prayers can be "hindered" (1 Peter 3:7). That statement should get the attention of every man!

God intended us to learn to love our wives and provide an atmosphere where they can grow spiritually and as individuals. This verse doesn't say they are always correct or that we are always correct. It does say that we are to provide this loving and honoring atmosphere where our wives will grow and be nourished.

Loving our wives and living with them in the way God desires requires us to pay careful attention to the state of our hearts and minds toward them. If we are dishonoring them in our hearts or thoughts, it will be difficult to convey honor and understanding with our actions and lives. If a husband is cruel, harsh, or condescending to his wife, God will take up her cause and begin to resist the husband. This could mean unanswered prayers, difficulty at work, or however God chooses to get our attention. He wants us to learn to love her, not crush her.

Guard Your Heart and Mind

We also need to discuss the importance of our thought life and guarding our minds, because, *"Above all else, guard your heart, for everything you do flows from it."* (Proverbs 4:23).

Realizing the importance of this admonition can be the difference between success and failure in life, between a great marriage and one that fails. This one thing affects all areas of our life, including our marriage. In another version, the above scripture in Proverbs says we must guard our hearts "with diligence" (4:23, NASB). In other words, guarding means a constant awareness not to allow anything that is unscriptural, unhealthy, or improper to take root in our hearts or minds, including our thinking patterns.

Regarding our wives, this means that we do not let unhealthy attitudes, critical attitudes, or anger take root in our heart. In addition, we do not allow fantasies or lustful thoughts of other women take root in our heart.

The Bible speaks of our heart as our "desire center." We have to be cautious about what desires we allow to take root in our hearts. Jesus said, *"For out of the heart come evil thoughts—murder, adultery, sexual immorality, theft, false testimony, slander. These are what defile a person; but eating with unwashed hands does not defile them"* (Matthew 15:19-20).

Jesus was pointing out that all unclean thinking starts in our thoughts and in our hearts. The thought may come from the evil one, the devil, or it may be something that is rooted in our own hearts. Satan knows that if he can get something into our hearts, it will grow within us and eventually play out in our lives. That is why we must guard our hearts.

We must see our hearts as the soil of our lives where seeds are planted that will take root and grow. We can control the seeds that are being planted and remove the weeds.

The Apostle Paul wrote, *"We demolish arguments and every pretension that sets itself up against the knowledge of God, and we take captive every thought to make it obedient to Christ"* (2 Corinthians 10:5). This means we have to guard against allowing our minds to entertain thoughts that are unhealthy, unscriptural, or that violate God's Word or character.

By the way, this is a battle we all face. No one is exempt. While some may battle in some areas, others battle in other areas. Jesus would not have told us we can overcome in this area if we couldn't. He wouldn't give us a command we cannot carry out. But this area requires prayer and practice.

As we pray over it and practice it, we get better at it. And if there are things in our heart that open the door to wrong thinking, as we pray about it God will help us and reveal to us what we need to do to overcome in this area. If He wants us to do it, He will help us do just that. You are not helpless or alone in this. He is with all of us and His Holy Spirit is with us to help us.

I would include here things that we imagine can happen or that we imagine are our wives' motivations or intentions. We can allow our minds to conjure up things that often are not true. As we dwell on these things, we can get angry or offended with our wives, or others, or even become discouraged or depressed about our circumstances. This is all because of entertaining thoughts we do not know are even true.

This doesn't mean we become naïve and unaware of what is going on around us. It does mean we do not allow our imaginations to take over and take up unjustified offenses toward our wives or anyone else. I have been guilty of this many times. I get mad about things only to find out either they didn't happen as I thought or didn't happen at all. I got all worked up over nothing! This happens to all of us and we must guard against it!

I can't tell you how many times I have built up a case against someone and then found out that what I thought was true, wasn't. It's a scheme of Satan to get us to entertain thoughts or take up offenses against someone when we do not even know if the thoughts we are entertaining are even true. We can get wound up and bound up at times for no reason at all. It is just speculation and vain imaginations.

If you do this, break this pattern. Every time you begin to think about things that accuse others (especially your wife) or cause you to take up an offense, stop thinking about it and instead begin to pray about it. Let God's peace come over you and cast off the stressful and divisive thoughts.

Remember, the Bible states that Satan is the accuser of all Christians (Revelation 12:10). He accuses us to ourselves, us to others, and others to us. He also accuses us to God the Father, trying to rob us of God's blessings on our lives. But God is faithful to us and His Word! So Satan will accuse others to us and we must learn to stand against it and not entertain these thoughts.

A good acronym is taking the word FEAR and using each letter to spell out the phrase: False Evidence Appearing Real. Satan certainly will fill our thoughts with lies and deceptions to rob us of our peace and get us to act in a manner that is motivated by fear, anger, lies and deception. It is important that we learn not to dwell on any negative thoughts, especially if we do not even know if they are true!

Satan's Accusations and Lies

As we said, Satan is the accuser of the brethren (Revelation 12:10). He accuses us to others and others to us—including our wives and children. He also accuses us to ourselves, making us feel guilty, useless, unworthy, and a failure. He brings up our mistakes and beats us up with them. He accuses anyone he can, anytime he can, about anything he can.

It is also how he brings division in a marriage. He will tell us false things about our wives and make us believe they have ill will toward us. Before you know it, we are mad for no reason at all. He's good at it; in fact, he's the best at it.

Be on guard against the accuser, his goal is to cause strife, conflict and division. His motives are not love, but hate. He wants to destroy our marriage and any other meaningful relationship in our lives. Don't let him!

Taking Thoughts Captive

When accusing thoughts come into your mind, regardless of whether they are about you or your wife, stop thinking them. Pray and begin to render your thoughts captive to Christ. Tell Jesus about the thoughts and give them to Him. If the Lord wants to convict us about something, He will do it without condemning us. He does it to bring us to repentance if needed, so we can be forgiven, healed, and encouraged. Satan does it to drag us down and discourage us.

God restores. Satan destroys.

If you find you have allowed unhealthy things to take root in your heart, confess them and ask God to forgive you. Like Jesus did, declare God's truth and tell the enemy to be gone from you (see Matthew 4:10). Remember that, as James tells us, the devil will flee when we do this: *"Submit yourselves, then, to God. Resist the devil, and he will flee from you. Draw near to God and He will come near to you"* (James 4:7, NIV). Receive God's forgiveness and don't walk in any condemnation. God is a compassionate Father who is slow to anger, quick to forgive, and happy to wipe our slate clean (Psalm 103:8-14).

In addition, from then on stand firmly against anything that is displeasing to God taking further root in you. You can choose to have a healthy heart or an unhealthy one. But, like a garden, it must be tended to be kept clean. *You* are in charge of your own mind and heart, your own garden! You own it, take care of it! It is part of your territory to rule over. You do not have to think about anything you do not want to think about. You have the ability to change and redirect your thoughts. In fact, the Bible tells us to do just that:

> *Do not conform to the pattern of this world, but be transformed by the renewing of your mind. Then you will be able to test and approve what God's will is—his good, pleasing and perfect will. (Romans 12:2)*

> *We demolish arguments and every pretension that sets itself up against the knowledge of God, and we take captive every thought to make it obedient to Christ. (2 Corinthians 10:5)*

> *Finally, brothers and sisters, whatever is true, whatever is noble, whatever is right, whatever is pure, whatever is lovely, whatever is admirable—if anything is excellent or praiseworthy—think about such things. (Philippians 4:8-9)*

Regardless of the source of the thoughts, as soon as we realize we are thinking about things we shouldn't, we should interrupt them and begin thinking about healthy things. When lustful or unhealthy thoughts enter our mind, ignore them. Just stop thinking about them and deliberately focus your thoughts on something else. If the thoughts seem to be intense and you are having trouble casting them off, then pray and ask God to break off the attack of the enemy who is attacking you. It is a spiritual battle. Pray and stand against it. It will go away as you do this. Then begin to think healthy thoughts.

Usually beginning to pray and thanking God, giving Him praise and thanking Him for His goodness, will break off the attack of Satan. Or, you can claim the authority of the name and blood of Jesus over your mind and thoughts. There is power in His name and in claiming the authority of His name and blood over us and our circumstances. We have authority over Satan by the work of Jesus through His death, burial, and resurrection, His work done for us. We need to claim that authority and stand against our enemy who accuses us and tries to rob us of God's blessings.

Note that the biblical example of how to address a lying spirit is by addressing it out loud. When the devil tormented Jesus with tempting thoughts, Jesus refuted the lies with scriptural truth and ended by simply telling him out loud to be gone, saying, "Away from me!" (Matthew 4:10). It is very effective for us to do the same.

When I realize the enemy is attacking me in my thought life, I begin to assert the name and blood of Jesus over my mind and against the enemy. The Bible tells us there is power in the name of our Lord Jesus. Since He has won the victory over Satan and his forces, it is in His authority that we can stand against them. His blood was shed for us; it washed away our sin (Revelation 7:14) and His shed blood provided our victory over sin and Satan. *"And they overcame him by the blood of the Lamb and by the word of their testimony, and they did no love their lives to the death"* (Revelation 12:11).

Speaking the name and the authority of Jesus against Satan and his forces is speaking out the very things that defeated them and which seal their fate eternally. When I do this, it is not often that the attack lasts more than a minute or two. In times when the battle is intense, I persist until the attack breaks off and the victory is won.

If taking your thoughts captive is an ongoing battle for you, it may be helpful to remember David's words as he battled the enemy giant Goliath. David said, *"The battle is the Lord's"* (1 Samuel 17: 47). We can certainly apply this attitude to our situation. God reminded the Israelite people as they went into what seemed an insurmountable confrontation with their enemy, *"Do not be afraid or discouraged because of this vast army. For the battle is not yours, but God's"* (2 Chronicles 20:15).

A heart that is trusting God is not fretting and worrying. Guarding what is planted in our hearts, casting down our imaginations, bringing every thought captive to Christ, and not allowing our hearts to dwell on negative things are all critical to the health of our marriage and our lives.

By the way, having impure thoughts enter our mind, or experiencing temptation, is not sin. The Bible states that Jesus was tempted in all ways as we are, but without sin. Satan is able to put thoughts in to our minds, but cannot read our minds. He will then condemn us and harass us for having the thoughts. The temptation is not sin; how we respond to the temptation, or the thoughts, is the test.

Grow in Honor

Honoring and understanding our wives is not compatible with entertaining negative thoughts about them. This doesn't mean we don't deal with a situation that needs our attention. But often, we get out of sorts because the enemy is feeding us thoughts, accusing our wife and family, and trying to get us angry with them when we don't even know if our thoughts are true. Don't become a victim of the "accuser."

Hopefully, these efforts to guard your thoughts and honor one another will be a mutual endeavor in every marriage. Both the husband and wife share the need to be honored and respected by the other. But as the leader in the home, we men should initiate—setting the example in thought and action, believing we will in turn receive respect and honor from our wives. If you do this, the seeds you sow in honoring your wife should bring a harvest of her giving honor to you in return. People tend to honor those who honor them. When a woman is loved, honored, and cherished, she feels secure in the marriage relationship and will begin to grow and develop into the person she is capable of becoming.

QUESTIONS FOR REFLECTION AND DISCUSSION

1. How do you honor your wife?

   _____

   _____

   _____

   _____

2. Do you see her as loved and valued by God? If so, do you love and value her as a "joint heir" of Christ? How do you demonstrate this? If this area needs work in your thinking and perceptions, how do you sense God speaking to you about this?

   _____

   _____

   _____

   _____

3. What qualities has God designed in your wife that make her uniquely her? What skills and talents stand out to you that you admire and appreciate most—and how can you affirm and support these?

   _____

   _____

4. What types of negative thoughts about your wife's motivations or actions do you tend to battle in your thought life? What do you purpose to do to begin to reclaim your thought life?

5. What types of thoughts about other women, if any, do you battle? How will you begin to reclaim these thoughts?

TAKE A KNEE

If you are having a battle with your thoughts, it's time to begin to reclaim your mind and thoughts. Let's pray, *"Father, I realize Your Word tells me I am not to think on things that are sinful, hurtful, and unhealthy. I ask You now to begin to show me how to reclaim my mind and thought patterns. I realize You would not tell me to do this unless it was Your will and possible for me to do so. I ask Your Holy Spirit to begin to empower me to walk in purity of thoughts. Please teach me how to do this and prompt me to pray about this as often as I need to in order to achieve this in my life. I want to give my wife honor and understanding as I live with her, and to ensure she feels valued and significant. As You cleanse and change my thoughts, increase my ability to live with her, and love her as You would have me to."*

Chapter 4

A Husband's Leadership and Authority

This part has a lot of people on each side of the issue. There is a part of our nature that does not like to submit to authority and be told what to do. So when we talk of a husband's role of leadership in the home, it brings up caution and even fear. However, we need to look to Scripture and what God has to say about husbands and wives.

God has designed His Kingdom to function within the context of godly order and structure. The Trinity functions this way: God the Father, Son, and Holy Spirit living in perfect selfless love and unity, and—at the same time—perfect, selfless, loving authority and submission. Jesus submitted to God the Father, although the Bible says He was equal with God the Father. He did it willingly out of love because it was the Father's will and Jesus wanted to please the Father. This is the model for the Church to follow, as well as the human family (see Ephesians 5, Titus 2, and 1 Peter 3).

God has ordained order and structure in the home as well. He places this "mantle" of leadership on the husband (in the Bible, a mantle, or cloak, could symbolize a responsibility or calling), and also is prepared to give him the grace and strength to carry that mantle of leadership.

Unfortunately, in our society, the whole concept of a husband's leadership and authority is controversial and often resisted. However, we need to look to God, the maker of men and women, and His Word, and seek His wisdom in this area.

Has there been abuse in this area? Yes. Have men abused their wives, physically or emotionally, and misused their leadership? Yes. However, the fact that there has been abuse in this area does not take away from God's truth and intentions.

Certainly, it is not God's will for anyone to be abused or taken advantage of. His plan is to bring order, peace, and love into the marriage relationship. Finding His plan for marriage is the key, not quoting cases of those who have been hurt by abusive husbands as a reason to disagree with God's Word. (By the way, I have also known some abused husbands.)

Husbands' personalities vary from a strong dominant leader to a more submissive personality willing to let his wife lead, and everything in between. Wives vary from being willing to follow their husband's leadership to resisting anyone and anything trying to lead them, and everything in between.

Often there are reasons people resist leadership and authority. Abuses suffered in the past can cause not only caution, but fear and strong resistance to authority and leadership. If a woman is in an abusive relationship, talking about submitting to a person who is abusing her cannot only be discouraging, but possibly more than she can handle. Again, God is not in favor of anyone being abused. Leadership leads and can be strong and firm, but not abusive.

Obviously we want to protect ourselves from abuse. This is normal. Personalities vary, but the Bible's teaching on order in the home is consistent regardless of the personalities of the couple. Each couple may handle this dynamic somewhat differently, but it is important that we understand what the Bible teaches.

God's Government in Marriage

God has established an order in the marriage relationship. Just as no company or country can be in order without leadership and healthy structure, neither can the marriage relationship.

The husband's role is to lead in love and set the tone and family culture for a healthy family. He is to exercise his leadership in an attitude and posture of unconditional love.

> *Follow God's example, therefore, as dearly loved children and walk in the way of love, just as Christ loved us and gave himself up for us as a fragrant offering and sacrifice to God. . . . Submit to one another out of reverence for Christ. . . . Husbands, love your wives, just as Christ loved the church and gave himself up for her to make her holy, cleansing her by the washing with water through the word and to present her to himself as a radiant church, without stain or wrinkle or any other blemish, but holy and blameless. In this same way, husbands ought to love their wives as their own bodies. He who loves his wife loves himself. (Ephesians 5:1-2, 21, 25-28)*

> *Husbands, in the same way be considerate as you live with your wives, and treat them with respect as the weaker partner and as heirs with you of the gracious gift of life, so that nothing will hinder your prayers (1 Peter 3:7)*

The wife, for her part, is asked to respect and submit to her husband's leadership.

Likewise, wives, be subject to your own husbands, so that even if some do not obey the Word, they may be won without a word by the conduct of their wives, when they see your respectful and pure conduct. (1 Peter 6:1-2)

God's desire is that wives willingly submit to the leadership of their husbands. A woman's motivation should not be because she thinks she is inferior to him (or because her husband believes she is inferior). The issue of a wife's submission is not one of a husband being superior, but rather a God-given order that brings God's peace and blessing into the home. Her actions are an act of faith, believing that God will honor her and work on her behalf if necessary. It is also done to bring harmony into the home.

Submit to one another out of reverence for Christ. Wives, submit yourselves to your own husbands as you do to the Lord. For the husband is the head of the wife as Christ is the head of the church, his body, of which he is the Savior. Now as the church submits to Christ, so also wives should submit to their husbands in everything. (Ephesians 5:21-24)

This is a picture of love and mutual respect, of giving and deferring to each other as needed. The wife is to love and respect her husband and to defer to his leadership. The husband is to love and honor his wife, living with her in an understanding way. Two people, each insisting on having their own way, will not produce harmony or a loving atmosphere in the home. On the other hand, two people lovingly submitted to the Lord and each other (Ephesians 5:21, 33), loving and respecting and honoring one another, will.

How a Husband Leads

Authority or leadership can be used or abused and always comes with responsibility. The authority to lead means God is also giving responsibility to the husband to lead in love and to lead in a responsible and biblical manner.

The husband has this responsibility whether he accepts it or not. He also has it whether his wife accepts it or not. Husbands, if we lead our wives in the manner in which Scripture commands us to, we make it all the easier for them to follow our leadership.

First, our responsibility is to treat them in an understanding way. Giving them honor and loving them is not contingent on the degree to which we "feel" respected. The husband is responsible to the Lord to lead with understanding and love regardless of his wife's response. It is not his responsibility to enforce respect and submission; that is an attitude of the heart between the wife and God.

It *is* a husband's responsibility to exercise leadership in such a way that your wife knows you love her and want only what is best for her, your family, and your marriage. A man can be both a strong and loving leader. He can be both bold and gentle. Jesus certainly was, and He is our example.

He showed love, compassion, mercy, and grace. He also spoke the truth and did not shrink back from dealing with those who needed it. To be like Him is our goal and we need to realize that to be like Him is not just a decision. It is allowing God to work in our lives to make us like Him.

Second, it is not God's plan for a man to ask his wife to do things that are sinful or inappropriate. As we saw in Ephesians 5:22-24, the wife is to submit to her husband. However, note that she is to submit to her husband "as to the Lord" (verse 22). This means she cannot commit sin nor act inappropriately, even if her husband asks her. Colossians 3:18 says, "Wives, submit to your own husbands *as is fitting in the Lord*" (emphasis added).

For example, for a man to ask his wife to view pornography or partake in other sinful acts is not "fitting in the Lord." She must decline. As well, asking—or worse yet, pressuring—your wife to do things that are unethical or illegal is wrong, and she should decline. At that point, she is deferring to the greater authority of God and trusting Him to support her. You need to honor her stand for what is right in these cases.

Third, the authority God gives a man in marriage does not allow for abuse of his wife or children, whether physically, emotionally, or verbally. If a husband abuses his wife, it is wrong in every sense. Depending on the abuse, she may have to remove herself from the relationship, praying that God will change her husband and bring him to repentance.

Finally, leading in an understanding way means we don't exercise authority in a vacuum of relationship or counsel. Ephesians 5:21 reminds us that we are to submit to "one another out of reverence for Christ." As the Trinity functions in perfect equality of value and personhood, while at the same time distinct in role and authority, so should we. One is not better than the other, just different. And we are not to function independently of one another.

As mentioned earlier, your wife has talents and abilities you do not have. She also has spiritual gifts you do not have. She will be able to do things well that you cannot. She will also have a different viewpoint and perspective on situations. Remembering this, and seeking her counsel as you make decisions, is wise and appropriate.

It is perfectly appropriate—and desirable—that a wife should give her husband counsel, especially if she is alarmed about an upcoming decision. If there is a problem in the relationship, and she does not talk to him about it, he might go on thinking all is well. A godly wife will let her husband know when she disagrees with him, though she can do this in a respectful way.

Yelling and screaming is never productive. If she strongly disagrees, she should tell him and encourage prayer over matters of concern. If, after she voices her concern, her husband decides against her counsel, then she will have to trust God with his decision and the outcome. At this point she should pray and ask God to get involved and leave it up to Him.

I personally have gone against my wife's counsel many times and have had to live with the consequences. Often my actions were motivated by pride or by thinking I was right and she just didn't understand. While she may not have understood the details of a situation as well as I, in her spirit she was uncomfortable—and she turned out to be right. I had the facts, but her lack of peace was correct.

Right before the economic downturn in 2006, I sold my share of the company I had started to my partner, and then determined to start up again. I started looking for office space. I had everything planned out—how large of a space I needed, where it needed to be, how many offices I would need, and who would occupy the offices. I chose an excellent location and began to pursue a lease.

Joan however, encouraged me to look at other locations with much cheaper rent. I told her the reason why I had chosen my course and did not heed her counsel. After all, I had been a division president of the largest home builder in the USA and knew what I needed. Three years later, I was trying to get out of the lease and the three years ended up costing $400,000. If I had listened to Joan, this would not have happened.

Men, if your wife is telling you she feels strongly about something, you should listen and consider what she is saying. God may be using her to caution you. Many times God speaks to us through our wives. We should never assume we are right and she is wrong. Obviously, all decisions should agree with Scripture. But, the Bible tells us to seek counsel (Proverbs 11:14). A man who is unwilling to seek godly counsel—including that of his wife—will be headed for a fall.

Marriage is both a partnership and should be biblically ordered. I consider my wife my life partner. We discuss things and make decisions together, as we should. We pray together about important decisions and seek God for His guidance. We are in this together for the long haul.

My decisions affect Joan and our family and it is appropriate and practical that we should discuss our decisions and direction. We are a team and I value her, her input, her talents and contributions, and her viewpoints. If she doesn't feel right about something, I need to listen to her. God's Spirit is in both of us as Christians and He speaks to both of us and through both of us. Together we are stronger than apart.

What Does Leadership in the Home Look Like?

We have already discussed a man taking responsibility for his attitudes and actions. A husband's attitude toward his wife and family will determine the family culture and how the family will fare. Together they establish their family culture and atmosphere. A woman's nurturing skills and God-given aptitudes for the family play an important role in family life.

The first way a man should take leadership in the home is to make his own relationship with God a personal priority.* Following are some other ways a man can lead:

Seek God's wisdom. We should always begin with seeking God for His wisdom on how to lead. Remember, God wants your family to be healthy and productive. He knows the heart of each member and His plan for each. So, when you reach out to God, your Father, you are reaching out for the wisdom God

---

* See the study in this series, *Seeking and Finding God* for more information on this topic.

wants to give you. Who better knows your family and each member than Him?

He knows His plan and purpose for each of you. He wants you to seek Him so He can reveal His heart about your family to you. He wants to be involved in your marriage and family. Remember James 1:5, *"If any of you lacks wisdom, let him ask of God, who gives to all liberally and without reproach, and it will be given to him."* God promises to give wisdom to those who ask for it.

What are some of the things in which you might look for God's guidance and wisdom? Consider asking Him how to go about leading in the following areas:

- Regular family time
- Studying and applying Scripture
- Family prayer time
- Recreation time
- Vacations
- Church attendance
- Teaching, training, and discipling children
- Use of money
- Time management
- Your career and direction
- Life direction

These are not necessarily in order of importance and they are only a sampling of the arenas in which a husband can and should demonstrate leadership. All of these areas are very important to the family and the husband should take initiative, and along with his wife, decide how these things will be handled. This list may look imposing, but the key is simply doing them, not being perfect at them—no one is. Practice makes perfect, or at least improves us. Since a husband and wife are a team, these important family matters should be approached as a team effort.

Facilitate getting things done. A good leader gets things done. He takes on the tasks he should do and delegates or defers to others in areas where they are gifted. A good leader recognizes who is best able to accomplish things and delegates those things to them and then supports them in their efforts. He also wants to see those around him develop and grow. This is true of marriage—two people working together to take care of the family and family affairs.

A wise husband facilitates this by discussing things with his wife. Then they can decide together how they will accomplish the things to be done and who should be primarily responsible for the various household responsibilities. My wife can do some things much better than I, so I defer to her in those areas. A husband should not dump everything on his wife, or, conversely, have the attitude only he is capable of getting things done.

Reach agreement as a team. As we discussed earlier, the husband and wife are a team; each brings talents, abilities, and gifts. Decision-making in marriage is a team effort. When a husband and wife are in unity there is harmony and the family is blessed.

A husband and wife should be in agreement and back each other up. If a couple is not in unity and agreement, the children will know it and the family will suffer. After the husband and wife decide together who will take responsibility for important areas of the home and family life, then the other should be supportive. If the husband and wife do not work as a team, it will make success in these areas more difficult.

> ***A husband and wife who work together, pray together, and are unified in purpose make a powerful team.***

Identify problem areas and be proactive in reaching resolution when there is conflict. Talk about it with your wife; pray over it, and take the steps you can to reach resolution. Ignoring problems rarely solves them.

A HUSBAND'S LEADERSHIP AND AUTHORITY

Take a stand for what is right in your life, marriage, and family. When a wife knows her husband is a man of integrity and principle, her confidence in him grows. Your wife and children will know if you are a person of compromise or a person of integrity who stands for what is right.

Talk with and listen to your wife. Ask her questions about how she thinks and feels about life, your marriage, the family, your children, spiritual life, hopes and dreams for your future together, and so on. As you talk about and pray over these things, your intimacy will grow and your bond will become stronger.

Pray with your wife. We have already mentioned the necessity of praying with our wives; this is one of the most important things a husband can do as he leads. Statistics show that a husband and wife who pray together rarely get divorced. In fact, the divorce rate among couples who regularly pray together is less than one in 1,000 marriages. Compare that to the 50 percent divorce rate in our nation. Seeking God together brings God into the situation.

When we humble ourselves before Him and admit we need His guidance and direction, He responds. A husband and wife who can openly pray about their problems together, asking God with open hearts for His wisdom and solutions to whatever the problem or situation, will see God get involved. This cannot happen unless a husband sets aside time to pray with his wife.

This can be tough for many men. It requires us to open up to our wives before God and to pray about things that may be sensitive or difficult to admit. But there is power released from God when husbands and wives pray together.

Remember the unity and agreement principle: Prayer in agreement is powerful. Jesus said, *"Again, I tell you that if two of you on earth agree about anything you ask for, it will be done for you by my Father in heaven. For where two or three come together in my name, there am I with them"* (Matthew 18:19). A husband and wife praying together brings that power into the marriage.

You can pray about every area of your relationship: sex and intimacy, money, the children, problems between the two of you, the future, work, priorities, and whatever is important in life. Try setting aside time to pray with your wife at least weekly, if not more often. As you and your wife share what is on your hearts and pray about those concerns together, you will gain greater understanding of each other. You will end up "knowing" your wife in a much deeper and more intimate way.

I will never forget the first time I prayed with my wife. I had practiced having daily prayer and Bible study for years, but I did not pray with Joan. An older man who was mentoring or discipling me encouraged me to begin praying with her.

Initially it was difficult for me. I felt like I was opening up an area of my life that had been private. In fact, I *was* doing just that. However, the benefit was great. Joan and I became closer, more intimate, and able to share on a deeper level. She felt much more important to me as I opened up this part of my life to her. She in turn, was able to open up to me in new ways. The effect on our marriage was significant and positive. I can't say this enough: men, you need to pray with your wives.

When the Wife Doesn't Follow

Just as an overbearing, cruel, or hardhearted husband displeases the Lord and makes a marriage difficult, so does a wife who is contentious, rebellious, or wants to control her husband.

So, what if a wife will not accept her husband's leadership? It may be a matter of not understanding Scripture, or it may simply be a refusal to follow it. If this is the situation in your marriage, and your wife is willing to explore the issue with you, I suggest you do a Bible study together in 1 Peter 3, Ephesians 5, Colossians 3, and Titus 2. The fact that God addresses roles and family structure in four books of the Bible is significant.

If your wife is unwilling to be open to your leadership, I suggest you begin with prayer. Ask God to work in your wife's heart as you continue to lovingly lead her and your family. She might be afraid to submit to your leadership, fearing you will take advantage of her or just "blow it." Plus, there is much input from the world that tells her she should not do this; she should not give up her "identity" and her own mind. (By the way, God does not want her to lose her identity or her own mind or opinions, either!)

But a contentious wife hinders the family and marriage, violates God's order, creates a contentious atmosphere in the home, and brings grief to her husband. This dynamic will also have a great impact on the children. If this is your situation, you cannot abdicate your role of leadership and should provide leadership as you can.

If you have children, continue to lead and make the best possible decisions for them. As you pray for her, open yourself up to God and ask Him to change you in any needed areas. Often God wants to work on us first, then He will work on others in our lives. When there are problems in our marriages, we should be willing to seek God about us first, then our wives. We should bathe our wives and marriages in prayer. Especially when there are problems.

Men, we can be firm and decisive and do it with a loving heart and attitude. Remember, we are leading as we believe the Lord would have us to and doing what is best for our marriage and family. Jesus was not a weak leader. He spoke the truth and acted decisively. But He did all in love and always what was best for others. He is our example.

When the Husband Doesn't Lead

At times, a husband may find that leadership simply does not come naturally to him, which can create a vacuum in his home. I saw this in the marriage of a woman named Jean, who was a respected member of her church. She was a gifted teacher and viewed by all as a godly woman. She was a woman of prayer and a leader in women's ministries. Her husband, Gordon, was faithful in church, committed to his family, and liked by all.

In counseling, Jean shared that Gordon would not lead in the home. Jean was a natural leader, and Gordon was content to allow her to do so. He respected her walk with the Lord and looked up to her spiritually. However, she wanted her husband to "step up" and exercise leadership in the family. From her study of Scripture, she knew this was what God wanted and she wanted Gordon to develop into a family leader.

Jean was counseled to step back and let Gordon lead. When decisions came up, she was encouraged to give the decisions to him and do nothing until he had made a decision. Since this pattern of her leading had gone on for so long, she was encouraged to sit down with Gordon and tell him that she wanted him to lead and was going to defer to him from that point on.

When they had this conversation, Gordon nodded and agreed. Then the hard part came. Jean continually had to stop herself from taking charge. She needed to retrain herself to present Gordon with decisions and ask him to let her know what he had decided. Obviously she was willing to give her input. But in the past her input always became the decision. She wanted Gordon to think and act and take on leadership in the home.

It took awhile, but Gordon began to make decisions. Both of them had to work at it—Jean at deferring and Gordon at making the decisions, even though Jean might have felt more capable and been able to decide quicker. At times she disagreed, but I'm glad to say that Jean stepped back allowed Gordon to grow and learn from his decisions, right or wrong. Their marriage changed, their family changed, and their lives changed—all for the better. And since they had three sons, the sons' expectations of God's will for family structure changed.

Husbands, if you are married, God has given you the mantle of leadership whether you recognize it or not. It's up to you to learn to use it in a wise, practical, and loving manner as God intends. As in all areas of responsibility God gives us, He expects the husband to seek Him as to how to appropriately carry this mantle of leadership with his wife and children.

QUESTIONS FOR REFLECTION AND DISCUSSION

1. Were you aware that God has called you to lead in your home?

   _____

   _____

   _____

   _____

   If so, how would you evaluate your leadership?

   _____

   _____

   _____

   _____

   If not, how would you now state you understanding of that role?

2. If you haven't already done so, are you ready to begin to lead and assume the leadership role God has for you? What are some practical steps you can take to begin leading?

3. After reading this, are you convicted that you need to show leadership in other areas? Is so, what are they?

4. Have you discussed your leadership role with your wife? If so, what was the outcome? If not, what would you like to talk over with her?

5. Do you seek your wife's counsel? Does she know you value her input and counsel?

_____

_____

_____

_____

6. Do you pray with her about important decisions? If so, what has been the fruit of this practice in your marriage? If not, can you identify what is holding you back?

_____

_____

_____

_____

TAKE A KNEE

Let's pray: *"Father, I want to take up the mantle of leadership You have for me in my marriage and home. I accept the role of leadership as Your role for me. Teach me to wear that mantle in a loving and godly way. Help me understand what it means to lead, exercise authority, and love my wife in a way that blesses her and honors You. Put Your desires in my heart about this. I take this responsibility seriously and I welcome Your direction, wisdom, insight, and strength."*

Chapter 5

THE RESPONSIBILITY TO PROVIDE

Rick was a young man who had met his wife on a mission trip. He had been a part of a large mission organization and was convinced that he was to give his life to ministry. I was his pastor and he asked to meet with me. As we spoke, he shared his desire to be in ministry "full time" and to be involved in missions work.

When I asked him the type of work he was currently doing, he told me his wife was a nurse and worked to support them. They had no children and he stayed at home and waited for God to open up his ministry. I began to share with him that his first priority was to provide for his wife and seek how he could minister in the workplace until God opened up a possible position in vocational ministry, if that was His will.

I shared the great opportunities each man has to influence others in the marketplace, and that he has called all men to be priests and ministers of the Lord, not just those working in a church or on the mission field. Only a very small percentage of men are called to church staff or missions positions. However we are all God's priests, not just those in vocational ministry. I shared 1 Peter 2:9-10 with him:

> *But you are a chosen generation, a royal priesthood, a holy nation, His own special people, that you may proclaim the praises of Him who called you out of darkness into His marvelous light; who once were not a people, but are now the people of God, who had not obtained mercy but now have obtained mercy.*

Most men are called to "priestly" ministry in the marketplace, I explained, to be a witness and light there. This is not a lesser position in the body of Christ. God wants all men to be His ministers, to be a light and an influence wherever we are, especially in the market place.

Unfortunately, Rick could not accept this and thought I was discouraging him from believing God for "full-time ministry." I told him the higher priority was to align his life with Scripture. The Bible was clear; if he was unwilling to provide for his family, his life was out of order (see 1 Timothy 5:8). I told him it was very possible that he would begin to have marital problems as his wife could become disillusioned with their life. He got angry and left the meeting. I got a report two years later that his wife had left him and he was still trying to get into "full-time ministry."

The Bible teaches that a man is to provide for his family. Our first ministry is to our wife and family. We are not to neglect our family in order to minister to others or seek vocational ministry positions.

A man who seeks after God, and strives to honor Him in all he does is never a lesser man in God's sight than someone who may be famous or highly regarded.

If God wants a man to serve in vocational ministry, He knows where that man is and has no problem supplying the means to put him into that position. Our responsibility is to seek God, put Him first, take care of our families and other priorities, and allow God to build a message in our lives.

If it is God's will for us to discontinue secular work and pursue full-time vocational ministry, then He will open the door for this, and it will not be at odds with His other plans and commands for us.*

A Husband and a Wife's Work

The Bible teaches that men are to work and provide for their families. Both the husband and wife are a team to accomplish these things. But this raises the issue: Is it best for a mother who has children at home to work outside the home?

I want to share my perspective on this issue, although it may not be current with some people's thinking. Today, most women work outside of the home to help earn money for the family. They may be pursuing a career, or feel they have to work to bring in the money needed for the family. However, the Lord may have another plan for them. Let's consider what Scripture says (and doesn't say) about a man and his wife's responsibilities to provide for and raise up their family.

In Genesis 2:15 we read, *"The LORD God took the man and put him in the Garden of Eden to work it and take care of it."* Here

---

* This is discussed in greater detail in the book in this study, *A Man's Work and Ministry.*

we see that God established the concept of work and stewardship. The man was to work and tend the garden. God made it for man; man was to tend to it.

Then, in verse 18 of the same chapter we read, *"The LORD God said, 'It is not good for the man to be alone. I will make a helper suitable for him.'"* So God gave Adam a task to perform and then gave him a mate who was also his helper. Obviously, Eve was to work alongside Adam and help him in the tasks God had given him.

In Genesis chapter 3, we have the account of Satan, in the form of a serpent, deceiving Eve, and then Adam entering into sin with Eve by disobeying God. Thus, at that moment, sin entered the world and perfect fellowship with God was broken.

At this time, God spoke several things to Adam and Eve. He told Adam that he would have to work, and that his labor would begin to be hard (3:17, 19). He also established that Adam was to lead (have authority over) his wife, and that she would bear children in pain (3:16). Eve was to bear children, and Adam was to work and labor in the earth. This did not mean that Eve would not work alongside her husband, but that as the mother of their children she would have responsibility for the children and thus, the home.

In the New Testament, several verses discuss the roles of husbands and wives. In 1 Timothy 5:8 we read, *"Anyone who does not provide for their relatives, and especially for their own household, has denied the faith and is worse than an unbeliever."* The original manuscripts use the masculine pronoun in this passage, indicating that men are the "anyone" Paul is referring to who are to provide for their households.

In 2 Thessalonians 3:6-12, the Apostle Paul speaks on the themes of work and supporting ourselves. He says in verse 10, *"For even when we were with you, we gave you this rule: "The one who is unwilling to work shall not eat."*

Here again we see the biblical principle of working to support oneself. This can easily apply to both men and women. Each should do what they can to take care of themselves. This truth is repeated in 1 Thessalonians 4:11-12.

In Titus 2:4-5, Paul gives a command to the women of the church: "... *urge the younger women to love their husbands and children, to be self-controlled and pure, to be busy at home, to be kind, and to be subject to their husbands, so that no one will malign the word of God.*" Another translation renders "busy at home" as "workers at home."

In Old Testament times, the opportunities for women were much more limited than they are today. Certainly they are cases where women have been very successful in business. The Bible indicates that since women are the ones who bear children they are given gifts and abilities to nurture the family. During the years of childbearing, if a husband and wife decide that the wife is to be at home and oversee the home and raise the children, they should never feel this is a lesser position than working outside the home.

In Proverbs chapter 31, the godly woman is seen taking on many responsibilities, including buying fields, making clothing, and selling in the markets. She re-invests profits and buys a vineyard. She gives to the poor and reaches out to the needy. This chapter certainly shows a multi-talented woman who is hardworking, wise, compassionate, savvy in business, and full of good works both to her family and to the community.

One thing should be noted: This woman is working in her husband's estate. He is a man of means and is "known" in the gates, where he sits among the elders of the land (verse 23). The gates of the city were where important decisions were made and business transacted. Prominent and wise men were there to oversee these transactions and to lead in making decisions that affected the community.

This prominent woman was not neglecting her family, but was industrious working in her and her husband's estate—her home. She was obviously in charge of much including the household, servants, and work on the estate.

In summary, both men and women should have good work ethics. Both have responsibilities and work to do. When there are small children at home, work decisions should be made that build up the family and make raising, teaching, and training the children a priority.

If a woman can be at home during these years, it will be a blessing to the family and the marriage. The issue is where a woman's time is *best* spent considering her family. This is a decision each couple must make.

Early in our own marriage, my wife and I struggled financially. We both came from families of modest means and had little when we married. I was a college student, working part time, and Joan was an executive assistant for a small company. Between the two of us, we were making just enough to get by.

When I left school, and we had our first child, we had to make a decision. I was convicted that Joan should be at home with our children and that I was to believe God to bless my work. This kept me on my knees a lot, but forced me to grow in my faith and dependence on Him.

God always supplied. I learned to seek Him, to give financially, and to work diligently. As I grew in Him, my work began to be blessed and we, in turn, were blessed financially. We saw God's faithfulness to supply for us. It was a life lesson based upon God's will and us taking a stand we believed was scriptural and that God wanted for our family. *God is faithful.*

This is not to say that women cannot be successful in the workplace. Women can and do apply their talents, gifts, and abilities in the workplace. I have had many capable and talented women work for me whom I valued greatly. They made significant contributions to the success of our work.

The issue is the responsibility and priority of raising, nurturing, and taking care of children. When children are in the home, especially when they are young, they need attention, training, nurturing, guidance, correction, instruction, and love. While others can help in the endeavor, it is the parents' primary responsibility.

While both parents share in this responsibility, the issue is what is best for the children and the family. A husband and wife should pray about this and make these decisions with counsel and prayer. They are important decisions and will affect the family. A couple with children should not make decisions to conform to the world, but as God leads and directs.

I have known many women who are able to work from the home and who do well financially. As an employer, I work in an industry where women do well and some of my most valuable employees are women. They are talented, work hard and contribute greatly to the success of the business. I hope I am clear in stating that the issue is not ability, capability, or talent. But our responsibility and first priority is to raise our children in a loving and nurturing home and to teach them the ways of God and His Word.

The Benefit of Responsibility

One thing I mention cautiously and respectfully: in some cases, a wife working when children are at home may take the responsibility and need off the husband to develop and become the man God wants him to be. It could, in the long run, actually be a hindrance to his development.

The pressures of life can make or break us. God wants us to feel the need to seek Him and see Him work in our lives. He uses our responsibilities to motivate us to seek Him and grow spiritually.

Remember the saying, "No pain, no gain?" Maybe the Christian man should say, "No pressure, no growth." God uses responsibility to mold us. Having to be on our knees about responsibilities and how to fulfill them is not negative; it is positive.

Pressure in and of itself can be bad. Pressure that motivates us to seek God and learn to trust Him can be very positive. God does, and will, lead us into situations where we really need Him to come through. He wants us on our knees seeking Him. Then He wants us to marvel as He answers our prayers and comes through for us.

I'm not speaking of foolish decisions and reckless abandon. I'm talking about normal life. The goal in life is not to avoid responsibility. It is to run to God, cast our cares on Him, and see Him work in our lives and be faithful to us.

God will uses a man's work to develop him, stretch him and cause him to grow as a person. More importantly, He wants us to see Him be active in our work life.

Seek God about your work and pray over it. Ask God to help you and bless you there. Leading your family, working at your profession or job, and providing for your family are great challenges. As you seek God in these responsibilities, God will give you insight, shape your character, and develop a godly heart and mindset in you.

QUESTIONS FOR REFLECTION AND DISCUSSION

1. Do you take the role of provider for your wife and family seriously? If so, how are you currently needing to trust God to work through you to provide for your family?

2. God works through our work to develop Christlike character in us. How is God doing this in your life?

3. Have you discussed this area with your wife? Have you prayed with her about it? What is your direction is this area?

TAKE A KNEE

Let's pray over this area. *"Dear Father, I want to provide for my family. Teach me how to excel in my work. Show me how to be the best and most productive employee or worker I can. Give me vision for my work, my job, and my role to be a light to those around me. Help me to accomplish all You have for me in my work life. Show me the areas You are working on in my life through my work."*

Chapter 6

DIVORCE AND MARRIAGE

Divorce is a tough issue, and is prevalent in the Church as well as in the secular world. Many have been affected by divorce both inside and outside of the Church. However, we need to look at the Bible and see what God says about divorce and make that our conviction, not what the world says or what is happening and commonplace in the world around us.

If you are divorced, please read this entire section prayerfully with an open heart. Since divorce is hurtful and emotions are deeply involved, it can be a very sensitive topic. My desire here is for us to look to God for direction, and draw wisdom from His Word

My wife and I were fortunate to be brought up in homes where our moms and dads modeled marriage as a permanent union. My parents were married at age 16 and 19, really young. When my Dad died at age 90, they were still in love and loved being together. Like all people do, they had problems to work through and went through some tough times. But they stayed together, prayed together, and never considered divorce an option. Both Joan's parents and my parents grew in their relationships and in their love for each other over the years of their marriages.

Unfortunately, this high standard and deep commitment to marriage has been largely ignored or discarded in most societies today. High rates of divorce have become a reality in most Western nations. The "sexual revolution" of the 1960s, which has continued up to current times, has caused the divorce rate to skyrocket. The divorce rate in 1960 was 24 percent. Today is it 54 percent. Our nation has suffered from this.

Today's cultural emphasis is on pleasure and self-interest. Many would say "Life is short, and people need to make the most of it." A Christian should say, "Life is short, and we want to please God with our lives and discover His best for us."

The emphasis has become to try and find the perfect mate or "soul mate." Regrettably, it has become acceptable to pursue multiple attempts at finding the "right one." If the first marriage does not live up to expectations, many people simply try another. However, as they soon discover, subsequent marriages have their own problems. There is no "perfect" person and no perfect mate.

For a Christian, "making the most of life" means following God's plan for his or her life, including marriage. Let's look at what God's Word says.

God's Best for Marriage

The Bible mentions only two grounds for divorce: desertion and unfaithfulness. Jesus said,

> It has been said, "Anyone who divorces his wife must give her a certificate of divorce." But I tell you that anyone who

> *divorces his wife, except for sexual immorality, makes her the victim of adultery, and anyone who marries a divorced woman commits adultery. Again, you have heard that it was said to the people long ago, "Do not break your oath, but fulfill to the Lord the vows you have made." (Matthew 5:31-33)*

First Corinthians 7:15 speaks of marriage, stating that if a man or woman is deserted by his or her mate, then he or she is free to remarry. God set this high bar as His standard for marriage. It shows the importance He places on the marriage relationship. God also knew that men and women would get divorced. People fail and fall short. Marriages fail and fall short.

Satan and the world system have caused society to rob men and women of the joy and blessings marriage was intended to bring. The relationship God intended has been lost and replaced by any number of philosophical viewpoints, most of which are unscriptural and far less than God's best. God intended for marriage to be a blessing and a source for love, joy, intimacy, pleasure, mutual support, and companionship. Unfortunately, the world system—through Satan's lies and false values—has corrupted God's purpose.

Most marriages that fail do so for a number of reasons. Often, it is because they are not being lived as God intended. Many, if not most, struggling marriages among Christians can be saved. Some cannot because of the issues involved or because one or both partners are unable or unwilling to take the necessary steps to save it. It takes two to make a successful marriage. Both have to want a great marriage and willing to do the things that will make their marriage great. This is not always the case.

Jim was a man I knew whose marriage was in trouble. During a counseling session, he told me about his dissatisfaction. I listened to him describe the problems and noted the indifference he displayed toward his wife. Finally, he stated that he was just not happy with his marriage and didn't see any way to reconcile it. There *were* some genuine problems, but none that could not be overcome. His wife was devoted to him, had always been faithful to him, and wanted the marriage to work.

When I asked Jim if he would reconsider, he said no. I shared with him that there was great hope the marriage could not only be reconciled, but could become a great and satisfying relationship. Since God wanted the marriage to be successful, He stood ready to help them and transform their marriage.

When I explained God's plan for marriage and how Jim should stand for his marriage, praying over it daily and asking God to intervene, he said he just wanted out. He gave no compelling reason; he just wanted the marriage to be over. Unfortunately, he decided the effort was not worth it. Though he claimed to be a Christian, his attitude was one the world supports—*This one isn't what I want, so I will try another.* This is not God's desire.

Most couples married in a traditional ceremony take vows that say, "Till death do us part." These vows are not just between a man and a woman, but also are made before God and to God. As previously stated, it is a three-part ceremony between a man, a woman, *and* God. And, more than simply a ceremony, it is a covenant between those three parties. God is the one who created marriage and blessed it. In the marriage ceremony, a man and woman should recognize they are vowing to one another and God, and are entering into a relationship He established and wants to bless. They exchange vows to one another, before God, that are meant to be lifelong. No one should take this lightly. God certainly does not take it lightly.

The prophet Malachi spoke to the Israelite's about God's displeasure over their attitude toward marriage and divorce:

Another thing you do: you flood the LORD's altar with tears. You weep and wail because He no longer pays attention to your offerings or accepts them with pleasure from your hands. You ask, "Why?"

It is because the LORD is acting as the witness between you and the wife of your youth, because you have broken faith with her, though she is your partner, the wife of your marriage covenant. Has not the LORD made them one? In flesh and spirit they are His. And why one? Because he was seeking a godly offspring. So guard yourself in your spirit, and do not break faith with the wife of your youth.

"I hate divorce," says the LORD God of Israel, "and I hate a man's covering himself with violence as well as with his garment," says the LORD Almighty. So guard yourself in your spirit, and do not break faith. (Malachi 13:13-16)

These are strong words! The place marriage has in God's plan for mankind is significant. A man and woman should enter into marriage carefully and prayerfully, and not leave it easily.

Choice Points and God's Grace

Granted, a difficult marriage can wear a person down. Any difficult circumstance can do that. However, a difficult marriage is there every day, and has to be dealt with. Like most difficulties in life, it brings us to a point of decision: give up or seek God for His solution.

With this in mind, take a moment to read Matthew 19:3-12 in your own Bible. In this passage, Jesus deals with the topics of marriage, divorce, and the permanence of marriage. Notice that when Jesus explains that marriage is lifelong and permanent, even his disciples say, *"If this is the situation between a husband and wife, it is better not to marry"* (verse 10). It's good to see the human side of the disciples. Perhaps their own marriages might not have been all they wanted them to be at that point. Regardless, Jesus taught that it is not God's plan or desire for marriages to end in divorce.

In this world, however, there is often a conflict between God's plan and purpose for marriage, and our human views and experiences. Man looks at marriage in the natural realm—at circumstances and what seems to actually happen in life. But God knows His divine plan and purpose for marriage; He looks at life according to His plan and what is best for us.

It may seem to some that God's standard for marriage is humanly impossible to maintain in this world; therefore, it is not relevant. However, God does not make mistakes. He knows how He made men and women and His purpose for them. Through His Word and through His power—when we understand and apply them—we find that His plan and promises for marriage *are* possible.

One of the great problems in the Christian life is not understanding and knowing God's love and grace poured out through Jesus. When we do not feel loved, when we do not understand God's grace, it is difficult to love and extend grace to another. Realizing, experiencing, and living in God's love and grace transforms a person. That person will have the ability to love another in a greater and deeper manner.

When we experience great love and grace from God, we are able to give far greater and more meaningful love and grace to our mate. We can be a channel of God's love for him or her, and the fruits of the Spirit spoken of in Galatians chapter 5 will become real in our lives. Two people, experiencing God's love and grace, and channeling that toward each other, will have an exciting and meaningful marriage. You can have that type of marriage.

Abusive Marriages

One type of marriage that absolutely violates God's standard is one where there is abuse—whether physical, mental, or emotional. These marriages are difficult to reconcile.

Obviously, in these cases the abuser must have a genuine change of heart in order for there to be a basis for love and the plan God has for marriage. And the one being abused must give a lot of forgiveness and grace for there to be any hope of reconciliation. Sometimes through prayer and intercession, the abuser can change.

It is not God's will for anyone to be abused or to stay in an abusive relationship. Most often it is the wife, who is weaker physically, who gets abused. If this is the case, she might have to remove herself and her children from the relationship and get help and protection.

Men have no right to abuse their wives or children. Where this is the case, they must realize their actions are a sin toward their family, and a sin God hates, as people are getting hurt. Men, God wants you to love your wives, cherish them, and pray for them. They are to be your life partner, your best friend, your lover, and your confidante.

Can God heal an abusive marriage? Yes! But all must be open to Him and seek Him for transformation. Godly counsel may (and likely will) be required for this to happen.

Dealing with a Past Divorce

This is another area in which marriages today frequently struggle. As we have seen, divorce is not God's will or His best for marriage. However, divorce is a reality in our society and in the Western Church. If you are divorced, please do not be discouraged or feel condemned. God's love does not stop because a person gets a divorce. Read on, there is still much to be learned and applied from the Bible's teaching on, and God's design for, marriage.

First, realize that a divorce that occurred prior to you accepting Christ as your Savior is part of your past as an unbeliever. Praise God, our past mistakes and sins are washed away (1 John 1:9).

Perhaps you have experienced divorce since coming to Christ. There are many reasons why divorce occurs in Christian marriages. Sometimes a believer's spouse has an affair, or is determined to leave. At other times, life crises such as losing a child, going through bankruptcy, or other harsh or difficult circumstances can cause some to lose hope. In turn, they lose their faith that God can see them through their circumstances. Some marriages fall apart at these low points.

While God's purpose is for the husband and wife to band together during such times and renew their love and determination to see the difficult circumstances through, many do not. Satan rushes in at such times and tries to ruin marriages and destroy families.

Joan and I have experienced some difficult times, as most have. We have experienced difficulties in our relationship, in our finances, and with others. We have been disappointed, hurt, disillusioned, betrayed, taken advantage of and lied about. What's new; many if not most, have experienced such things.

In our case, God was wanting us to respond to those things by seeking Him, finding out what He had to say about these things, and trusting Him with our present and future circumstances. These things could have broken us. At times we felt confused and unsure about what lay ahead. But as we sought God, He brought us through all circumstances, and our marriage and love for each other actually strengthened during these times, by God's grace. It could have ended differently.

If a divorce occurs, regardless of the reason or timing, we must realize that divorce hurts people and hurts families; that's why God hates divorce. But when we turn back to God and renew our faith and relationship with Him, He accepts us, forgives us, and gives us the strength and power to move forward in faith and obedience. His love and grace are always there for us.

If you have experienced divorce and you are seeking God and are open to His working in your life, the events of a past divorce may have created circumstances that you are currently dealing with. Let's take a brief look at some of the areas where there may be issues caused by a divorce, and how we can deal with them in a manner pleasing to God.

Relationship with Your Ex-Wife

Often, there are bitter feelings toward an ex. However, it is critical that a Christian man forgive his ex-wife for any wrongdoing on her part. If possible, the relationship should be reconciled. If you or your former mate have remarried, this does not mean more divorces so you and your ex-wife can remarry. It does mean forgiving her and reconciling at least to the point of being cordial, respectful, and, if possible, friends.

This may not be possible, as your ex may not be interested in reconciliation. However, even if this is the case, it is still your responsibility to forgive her before the Lord and ask Him to heal you, *and her,* of any past wounds.* Also, pray for her. She was your wife at one point and you loved her. If you have children, she is the mother of your children. Pray for her, your children, her relationship with Christ, and ask God to bless her life.

---

* For more information on how to do this, please study the book in this series, *Repentance, Forgiveness, and Restitution.*

Provision for your children

As a man, it is your responsibility to provide for your children. If your wife has remarried and your children reside with her, there is joint responsibility between you and your wife's new husband. When he married her, he should have been prepared to take on the responsibility of a stepfather. Regardless, you are the children's father and you need to spend time with them, love them, have relationship with them, and provide for them. As their father, it is important for you to have godly influence in their lives, and as possible, to teach and train them in the ways of the Lord. You may also need to admit mistakes regarding the divorce that have affected them and ask them to forgive you, in order to make restitution with them.

Responsibility for your past actions

If you were unfaithful, an unloving husband, or harsh or cruel in your former marriage, you need to ask for your ex-wife's forgiveness. This should be done in person, if possible. If she has remarried, you may have to do this in the presence of her husband.

Regardless, it is for your sake and hers so that healing can take place. To do this, you will have to humble yourself, admit where you were wrong, and ask forgiveness. Whether or not she asks you for forgiveness in turn for things where you felt she was wrong, you need to step up and make right any area where you failed her. God will help you do this. Purpose to do what He would have you to do.

Forgiveness for an unscriptural divorce

If you did not have scriptural grounds for divorce (i.e., unfaithfulness or desertion), and you initiated the divorce, you need to ask God to forgive you for divorcing your wife. God is forgiving, but we need to repent and ask forgiveness in order for His grace, forgiveness, healing, and blessing to be released in this area. We cannot brush our mistakes under the carpet and assume all will be well. As men, we must deal with our mistakes, past and present, and make things right as we are able.

Forgiveness and healing are important for all involved. God wants this and when you pursue it His grace will be upon you to help you. You don't have to wonder if this is His will; it is. There is forgiveness for wrongful divorce, but it is important we approach this in a scriptural manner and align our lives with Scripture and God's will. That releases God's favor, grace, and emotional healing.

QUESTIONS FOR REFLECTION AND DISCUSSION

1. How do you view a marriage commitment? If someone asked you to describe how God views marriage, what would you say?

   _____
   _____
   _____
   _____

2. In your heart, do you see your marriage as a lifelong commitment? How do you demonstrate this?

   _____
   _____
   _____
   _____

3. Are there any problems in your life or marriage that come to mind as you read this chapter, and that need to be dealt with? Please list them below, and use this as the foundation for prayer, and to ask God where He wants to change you or call you to action.

_____

_____

_____

_____

4. If you are divorced, have you reconciled with your ex-wife? If not, are you willing to? Review the areas we covered above. What do you need to "get right" with her?

_____

_____

_____

_____

5. If you have children with your past wife, are you caring for them physically, emotionally, and spiritually, as the Lord desires? If not, how does it need to change?

_____

_____

_____

_____

TAKE A KNEE

Let's kneel and pray about our commitment to our marriage. *"Dear Father, please teach me to love my wife as You desire, and as she needs to be loved. Make my heart a "one-woman" heart. Begin to show me any wrong attitudes I have toward my wife. Change my heart in these areas so that it can agree with Yours. I want to have an exciting, loving, and meaningful relationship with my wife. I ask You to begin to work in my life, and my wife's, so our relationship can be all You desire it to be."*

If you are single, pray: *"Prepare my heart for the woman you have for me. Work in my life to make me ready for her."*

If you have divorced, divorce is a tough issue and usually affects many lives. God wants to heal and restore all who are involved in a past divorce. He loves all concerned. Let's pray: *"Dear Father, it is my desire to have Your best for my life. I want Your blessing on me and I want to live my life according to Your will and Your word. Forgive me of my past divorce and for my failings. I receive Your forgiveness, Lord, and I declare my forgiveness toward my ex-wife. Restore me, heal me, and help me do all I need to do to help promote healing for all involved."*

A FINAL WORD

Marriage is to be an adventure between two people. It is meant to be a rich, loving, and deeply meaningful relationship in which we learn to love each other as no other.

If things are currently not that way in your marriage, begin with yourself. Seek God and pray over your marriage. Ask Him to show you, from His perspective, the problems you're facing. Ask Him for wisdom, insight, and understanding.

Pray for your wife as well. Ask God to make your relationship with her what He wants it to be, and to bring His power and wisdom into your marriage. You can't go wrong there. He has great plans for your marriage. Seek Him, trust Him, and obey Him. Your marriage can be great!

ABOUT THE AUTHOR

Lou Turner wrote *Living Life God's Way* out of his passion for men to discover God, and to get to know Him and what He has for them. This 13-book men's discipleship series is the culmination of Lou's own journey—a life of seeking God, studying His Word, memorizing Scripture and meditating on it, and practical experience with family, community, marketplace work, and Christian ministry. It also comes, by Lou's own admission, from life experiences of both successes and mistakes, as a result of both good and bad decisions.

Lou has headed ministries, written and taught workshops, classes, and seminars, and discipled dozens of men. Now, he has put into print the things he has learned to help other men along their path and journey.

Most of Lou's growing up years were spent in Detroit and its suburbs, where he was raised in a pastor's home. After attending several universities and receiving his degree from the University of Phoenix with a Bachelor of Science in Business Administration, he and his wife planted and pastored a church for three years. After that time, he felt the strong call of God into business.

Over the years, Lou has served in numerous senior executive positions with national and international companies in the real estate and oil and gas industries. As of this writing, Lou is still active in business with his own home building company. He has

ABOUT THE AUTHOR

been married to his wife Joan since they were 20. They have three children and 10 grandchildren and make their home in Phoenix, Arizona.

www.ingramcontent.com/pod-product-compliance
Lightning Source LLC
Chambersburg PA
CBHW021118080526
44587CB00010B/560